DICERATOPS
and Other Horned Dinosaurs
by Dougal Dixon

illustrated by
Steve Weston and James Field

PICTURE WINDOW BOOKS
Minneapolis, Minnesota

Picture Window Books
5115 Excelsior Boulevard
Suite 232
Minneapolis, MN 55416
877-845-8392
www.picturewindowbooks.com

Printed in the United States of America.

 All books published by Picture Window Books
are manufactured with paper containing at
least 10 percent post-consumer waste.

Library of Congress Cataloging-in-Publication Data
Dixon, Dougal.
Diceratops and other horned dinosaurs / by Dougal
Dixon ; illustrated by Steve Weston & James Field.
p. cm. — (Dinosaur find)
Includes index.
ISBN 978-1-4048-4016-4 (library binding)
1. Diceratops—Juvenile literature. 2. Ceratopsidae—
Juvenile literature.
I. Weston, Steve, ill. II. Field, James, 1959- ill. III. Title.
QE862.O65D5857 2008
567.915—dc22   2007044143

Acknowledgments
This book was produced for Picture Window Books
by Bender Richardson White, U.K.

Illustrations by James Field (pages 4–5, 13, 15,
17, 21) and Steve Weston (cover and pages 7, 9,
11, 19). Photographs: istockphotos pages 8 (Alan
Tobey), 16 (Mike Capps), 18 (Roger Whiteway),
20 (Gerri Hernández); bigstock photos 6 (Herbert
Kratky), 10 (Avraham Kushnirov), 14 (Chris Fowie);
Frank Lane Photo Agency 12 (Philip Perry).

Consultant: John Stidworthy, Scientific Fellow of
the Zoological Society, London, and former
Lecturer in the Education Department, Natural
History Museum, London.

Types of dinosaurs

In this book, a red shape at the top of a left-hand page shows the animal was a meat-eater. A green shape shows it was a plant-eater.

Just how big—or small— were they?

Dinosaurs were many different sizes. We have compared their size to one of the following:

Chicken
2 feet (60 centimeters) tall
Weight 6 pounds (2.7 kilograms)

Adult person
6 feet (1.8 meters) tall
Weight 170 pounds (76.5 kg)

Elephant
10 feet (3 m) tall
Weight 12,000 pounds
(5,400 kg)

TABLE OF CONTENTS

WHAT'S INSIDE?

Horned dinosaurs! These animals lived in many places in the prehistoric world. Find out how they survived millions of years ago and what they have in common with today's animals.

HORNED DINOSAURS

Dinosaurs lived between 230 million and 65 million years ago. There were lots of different kinds of dinosaurs. The horned dinosaurs grew horns on their heads and faces. Some of them had bony frills, or shields, that stretched from the back of their heads over their necks. The horned dinosaurs lived toward the end of the age of dinosaurs.

A herd of *Centrosaurus* migrated across the plains. Along the way, the herd passed groups of *Styracosaurus* and *Pachyrhinosaurus*.

GRACILICERATOPS

Pronunciation:
GRAS-i-li-SAIR-uh-tops

Graciliceratops lived in what is now Asia. It had a sharp beak, like that of a parrot, for nipping at plants such as ferns and conifers. A bony frill grew from the back of its head. Rather than stop and fight, *Graciliceratops* would run away or hide from dangerous predators.

Running away today

A modern hare runs quickly to escape from danger, just like *Graciliceratops* once did.

Size Comparison

Graciliceratops was always watching for danger. If trouble came near, it stood up and ran away on its back legs.

PROTOCERATOPS

Pronunciation:
PRO-toe-SAIR-uh-tops

Protoceratops lived in sandy wastelands. It was the size of a sheep and had a strong beak and jaws that it used to pick at and chew on tough desert vegetation. *Protoceratops* lived in large herds, which helped protect it from fierce hunters like *Velociraptor*.

Desert animals today

Like *Protoceratops* once did, the modern camel lives in the desert. The camel spends much of its time taking shelter from sandstorms.

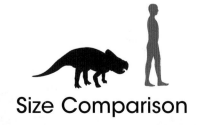

Size Comparison

Strong winds could have blown the desert sand around in dusty clouds, causing a herd of *Protoceratops* to seek shelter.

MONTANACERATOPS

Pronunciation:
mon-TAN-uh-SAIR-uh-tops

Montanaceratops lived in herds and fed on the sparse vegetation of open plains. The dinosaur had a short nose horn and a large, bony neck frill for defense. *Montanaceratops* pulled at and tore plants with a beak and chewed the plants with its teeth.

Living on plains today

Some modern breeds of goats eat the few plants found on desert plains, just as *Montanaceratops* once did.

Size Comparison

A group of *Montanaceratops* grazed on plants that grew on hot, dry plains.

Pronunciation:
SEN-tro-SAW-rus

Centrosaurus had a nose horn that may have been curved. *Centrosaurus* could have used the nose horn to dig up or scrape around for food. The dinosaur also had short horns that grew around the edge of its neck frill.

Ground scrapers today

Modern elephants use their tusks to scrape bark from trees, much like *Centrosaurus* did.

Size Comparison

Centrosaurus used a pointed nose horn to break bark away from a tree. It also used the horn to dig up tasty plants and roots.

STYRACOSAURUS

Pronunciation:
stie-RAK-o-SAW-rus

Styracosaurus was one of the strangest-looking of all of the horned dinosaurs. The animal had a horn on its nose and another six horns around the edge of a neck frill. All of the horns made *Styracosaurus* easy to pick out from the other dinosaurs.

Distinctive heads today

The modern hartebeest has horns that are different from those of any other antelope. Like the horns of *Styracosaurus* once did, the hartebeest's horns help animals recognize one herd from another.

Size Comparison

Running from a forest fire, a *Styracosaurus* mother protected the youngest member of the herd.

PACHYRHINOSAURUS

Pronunciation:
pak-i-RIE-no-SAW-rus

Pachyrhinosaurus was a large, horned dinosaur. The dinosaur's biggest horns were on a frill that stretched around the back of its head. *Pachyrhinosaurus* also had a big lump of bone on its nose. With the bone, the dinosaur rammed into other animals.

Head-butters today

Modern male buffalo often fight each other for their place in the herd, just like *Pachyrhinosaurus* did long ago.

Size Comparison

Pachyrhinosaurus males may have taken part in pushing contests to decide who was strongest.

DICERATOPS

Diceratops had two horns, one above each eye. The dinosaur also had a bony frill that stretched from the back of its head. The frill could have been used as a shield, but it definitely made the animal look bigger. With its frill and horns, *Diceratops* could both frighten and attack its enemies.

Head ornaments today

Modern deer have antlers that can be used for show and for fighting, just as *Diceratops'* shield once was.

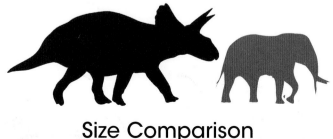

Size Comparison

When two *Diceratops* fought over territory, they used their horns and frills to battle for strength and power.

TRICERATOPS

Pronunciation:
tri-SAIR-uh-TOPS

Triceratops was the last of the horned dinosaurs. It was also the biggest. The dinosaur was big enough to fight one of the largest and fiercest meat-eaters—the mighty *Tyrannosaurus*. There must have been some terrible fights between the two of them!

Horns today

A modern rhinoceros has sharp horns that it uses to protect its young from a dangerous enemy, just like *Triceratops* once did.

Size Comparison

Triceratops had two long horns above its eyes and a small horn on the nose. The horns were used in defense during an attack from *Tyrannosaurus*.

WHERE DID THEY GO?

Dinosaurs are extinct, which means that none of them are alive today. Scientists study rocks and fossils to find clues about what happened to dinosaurs.

People have different explanations about what happened. Some people think a huge asteroid that hit Earth caused all sorts of climate changes, which caused the dinosaurs to die. Others think volcanic eruptions caused the climate change and that killed the dinosaurs. No one knows for sure what happened to all of the dinosaurs.

GLOSSARY

beak—the hard front part of the mouth of birds and some dinosaurs; also known as a bill.

ferns—plants with finely divided leaves known as fronds; ferns are common in damp woods and along rivers

frill—large piece of bone at the back of the head and over the neck of a horned dinosaur

herd—a large group of animals that moves, feeds, and sleeps together

horns—pointed structures on the head, made of bone

plain—large area of flat land with few large plants

predator—an animal that hunts and eats other animals

To Learn More

More Books to Read

Clark, Neil, and William Lindsay. *1001 Facts About Dinosaurs.* New York: Dorling Kindersley, 2002.

Dixon, Dougal. *Dougal Dixon's Amazing Dinosaurs.* Honesdale, Penn.: Boyds Mills Press, 2007.

Holtz, Thomas R., and Michael Brett-Surman. *Jurassic Park Institute Dinosaur Field Guide.* New York: Random House, 2001.

On the Web

FactHound offers a safe, fun way to find Web sites related to topics in this book. All of the sites on FactHound have been researched by our staff.

1. Visit *www.facthound.com*

2. Type in this special code: 1404840168

3. Click on the FETCH IT button.

Your trusty FactHound will fetch the best Web sites for you!

Index

LOOK FOR ALL OF THE BOOKS IN THE DINOSAUR FIND SERIES: